SCOOP
THE LITTLE HANDBOOK OF TRADITIONAL ICE CREAM RECIPES

NATASHA ZABOLSKY

Ivy Press

The book was conceived, designed and produced by

Ivy Press
210 High Street
Lewes, East Sussex
BN7 2NS, UK
www.ivy-group.co.uk

ISBN-13: 978-1-905695-64-5
ISBN-10: 1-905695-64-0

British Library Cataloguing-in-Publication Data
A catalogue record for this book is available
from the British Library

Creative Director **Peter Bridgewater**
Publisher **Jason Hook**
Editorial Director **Caroline Earle**
Art Director **Sarah Howerd**
Page layout **Kate Haynes, Richard Peters**
Senior Project Editor **Dominique Page**
Concept Design **Chris Harman**
Illustrations **Melvyn Evans**

Printed in China

10 9 8 7 6 5 4 3 2

SCOOP CONTENTS

THE INSIDE SCOOP

You probably think that home-made ice cream needs a lot of expertise and a big machine to churn it, whip it and generally perform the alchemy that turns it from a bunch of ordinary ingredients into frozen magic. It's true that there's a wide range of luxurious machines available that will make a delicious home-made ice. But ice cream can also be much, much less work than you might think. With only a freezer, a bowl and a whisk (or sometimes even a fork) you can make impressively delicious ices in almost any flavour you like, from classic vanilla to stem ginger, and from fresh strawberry to lemon meringue. You can also whip up pure and creamy ices fit for tiny children, or create exotic alcohol-spiked treats for sophisticates. Some need beating once or twice as they freeze, but just as many can be left entirely to their own devices once in the freezer, needing to be removed only when you're ready to eat them.

One of the joys of home-made ice cream is the purity of the flavours – they come through very cleanly, so even if you're someone who likes your ice cream with lots of crunchy or creamy additions, try some of the plainer options in the following pages, too – don't rush to complicate the flavour. You may be surprised by how delicious a strawberry ice made literally with only strawberries and cream is, or by the gorgeous texture of an absolutely plain chocolate ice. Equally, use the best ingredients that you can afford to buy: most of these recipes have a short list of ingredients that will allow the taste of organic fruit at the peak of its season, excellent-quality chocolate and pure flavouring extracts to really shine through.

Making these ices isn't complicated, but there are a few rules to follow. The ingredients usually include cream, but often also incorporate yogurt, eggs and sometimes milk, too. You need only basic equipment, although a stock of lidded 1-litre/1¾-pint freezerproof containers is necessary (a shallow, rectangular shape will freeze your ice cream more effectively than a narrow, deep one), and a spatula and an electric whisk will be very useful. Freezing times range from 3–6 hours.

Cream takes on other flavours easily – great when you're making the perfect chocolate ice, less good when you find that a bowl of cream has borrowed the flavour of the onion soup stored beside it in the fridge. Keep cream cartons sealed until you're ready to use them, and make sure that all utensils are scrupulously clean. Don't switch the types of cream around, and measure ingredients carefully. An ice with too much water in it may turn crystalline, whereas one with too little cream turns very solid, then melts to a mush without hitting a perfect in-between stage. A lot of the recipes contain raw egg – without a custard base, the egg white aerates the mixture and the egg yolk adds a crucial hit of richness – so pick and choose your recipes if you are feeding very small children or anyone who is pregnant or in fragile health.

Once you've mastered the perfect ice cream, try some of the other options, such as natural-juice lollies for a hot day, mango kulfi or one of the water ices or sorbets. The last chapter looks at accompaniments – from praline and sauces to help you construct a luxurious sundae, to a full-blown ice-cream layer cake.

Make only enough for one sitting: it's never a good idea to leave ice cream sitting around and then to refreeze it – although, frankly, this rule isn't likely to be a problem. Unless otherwise specified, most of these recipes will feed between four and six greedy but not gluttonous people, whether scooped lavishly into cones or spooned into bowls.

DO

• Use really good ingredients – with simple recipes, it's worth it.
• Measure liquids carefully – too much purée and the result may turn icy rather than creamy.
• Use the type of cream specified – full-fat, whipping, double and single creams each have their own role, and aren't interchangeable.

DON'T

• Increase quantities if you're using alcohol as a flavouring – too much can stop an ice cream from freezing properly.
• Keep removing ice cream from the freezer. Once made, freeze it for the time specified, then take it out to allow it to soften a little at room temperature before eating. Where the softening time is important, it's been included in the recipe instructions.

CHAPTER 1
CLASSIC ICE
CREAMS

A creamy selection of 15 top flavours, from pure vanilla to zabaglione, hazelnut and honey. Start with vanilla and strawberry – neither take more than 10 minutes to make – then branch out into something less obvious: a traditional but unusual brown-bread ice cream, for example, or a batch of the honey-flavoured ice cream, which tastes like the very essence of summer.

VANILLA

This is a smooth, delicious ice cream that not only makes a classic summer treat but can also form the base for countless variations. Because vanilla is such a pure taste, it's well worth searching out proper vanilla extract.

INGREDIENTS

2 LARGE EGGS
55 G/2 OZ CASTER SUGAR
300 ML/10 FL OZ DOUBLE CREAM
1-2 TSP VANILLA EXTRACT

METHOD

● Separate the eggs into 2 bowls. ● Beat the egg whites until stiff, then beat in the sugar, a spoonful at a time, until the mixture has formed a glossy meringue. ● In a separate bowl, whip the cream until thick but not stiff. ● Break up the egg yolks with a fork and stir them around a little, then add the vanilla extract to taste. ● Using a spatula, gently fold the whipped cream into the meringue. When it is almost incorporated, gradually fold in the egg yolks, a spoonful at a time. ● Pour the ice cream into a plastic freezerproof container and freeze for at least 6 hours or until solid. ● Remove the ice cream from the freezer and set aside for 10 minutes before serving.

PREPARATION TIME: 10 MINUTES
FREEZING TIME: 6 HOURS

12 CLASSIC ICE CREAMS

PURE BERRY

You can't get a purer ice cream than this – the only ingredients are strawberries, sugar and cream. Make it when the strawberry season is at its height and there's a glut of rich, ripe berries.

INGREDIENTS

450 G/1 LB FRESH, RIPE STRAWBERRIES
115 G/4 OZ CASTER SUGAR
300 ML/10 FL OZ DOUBLE CREAM

METHOD

● Hull the strawberries and cut each one into 4 pieces. ● Put the pieces in a bowl and stir in the sugar. Set aside for 2 hours. ● Transfer the strawberry mixture into a blender and blend until a thick purée forms. ● In a separate bowl, whip the cream until thick but not stiff. ● Using a spatula, fold the purée into the cream, then spoon the mixture into a plastic freezerproof container and freeze for 1½ hours. ● Remove the container from the freezer, stir well, then return to the freezer and freeze for another 4 hours. ● Remove the ice cream from the freezer and set aside for 15 minutes before serving.

PREPARATION TIME: 2 HOURS 10 MINUTES
FREEZING TIME: 5 HOURS 30 MINUTES

STRAWBERRY

This ice is stabilized by eggs, so you are not so reliant on very ripe fruit for the texture of ice. If you like your ice cream without seeds, sieve the purée before mixing it in with the cream.

INGREDIENTS

115 G/4 OZ FRESH STRAWBERRIES
85 G/3 OZ CASTER SUGAR
2 LARGE EGGS
300 ML/10 FL OZ DOUBLE CREAM

METHOD

● Put the strawberries into a blender with 25 g/1 oz of the sugar and blend until a purée forms. ● Separate the eggs into 2 bowls. Beat the egg whites until stiff, then beat in the remaining sugar, a spoonful at a time, until the mixture has formed a glossy meringue. ● In a separate bowl, whip the cream until thick but not stiff. ● Pour the strawberry purée into the egg yolks and mix together with a fork. ● Fold the whipped cream into the meringue, then fold in the strawberry mixture. ● Pour the mixture into a plastic freezerproof container and freeze for 5–6 hours. ● Remove the ice cream from the freezer and set aside for 10 minutes before serving.

PREPARATION TIME: 10 MINUTES
FREEZING TIME: 6 HOURS

CHOCOLATE

When you want a chocolate ice cream, you want it rich. This is a dark, luscious mix with a true chocolate flavour. It may be too rich for small children – in which case, try the chocolate-chip on pages 18–19.

INGREDIENTS

2 LARGE WHOLE EGGS AND 2 EGG YOLKS
115 G/4 OZ CASTER SUGAR
225 G/8 OZ PLAIN CHOCOLATE
300 ML/10 FL OZ SINGLE CREAM
300 ML/10 FL OZ DOUBLE CREAM

METHOD

• Put the whole eggs into a heatproof bowl and add the extra egg yolks. Add the sugar and beat together until the mixture is thick and pale. • Break the chocolate into small pieces and put it in a saucepan. Add the single cream and heat gently over a low heat until the chocolate has melted. • Stir the chocolate mixture into the egg and sugar mixture and mix together quickly but thoroughly. • Set the bowl over a saucepan of simmering water (or use a double boiler), making sure that the water does not touch the base of the bowl. Cook gently, stirring constantly, until the mixture has the texture of double cream. • Remove the bowl from the saucepan and leave to cool. • In a separate bowl, whip the double cream until thick but not stiff, then gently fold in the cooled chocolate mixture. • Pour the mixture into a plastic freezerproof container and freeze for 2 hours. • Remove from

PREPARATION TIME: 1 HOUR
FREEZING TIME: 6 HOURS

the freezer and beat thoroughly with a whisk or a fork, then freeze for another 4 hours or until solid. ● Remove from the freezer and set aside for 15 minutes before serving.

CHOC CHIP

This is an extremely simple ice cream and is usually very popular. It's a good one for children to help with as it takes only ten minutes to mix, from start to finish – although they'll then have to wait for 4 hours for it to freeze!

INGREDIENTS

225 G/8 OZ PLAIN CHOCOLATE OR 175 G/16 OZ PLAIN CHOCOLATE AND 55 G/2 OZ CHOCOLATE CHIPS
1 TSP HOT WATER
300 ML/10 FL OZ DOUBLE CREAM

METHOD

● If you are not using ready-chipped chocolate for your 'chips', roughly chop 55 g/2 oz plain chocolate into small pieces and set aside. ● Break the remaining chocolate into small pieces and put into a heatproof bowl set over a saucepan of simmering water. Add the hot water and leave until the chocolate has melted. ● Meanwhile, in a separate bowl, lightly whip the cream until thick but not stiff. ● Remove the chocolate from the heat, leave to cool for 1–2 minutes, then stir well and beat into the cream until well combined. ● Add the chocolate chips or chopped plain chocolate and mix together lightly. ● Pour the mixture into a freezerproof container and freeze for 4 hours or until solid. Remove the ice cream from the freezer and set aside for 10 minutes before serving.

PREPARATION TIME: 10 MINUTES
FREEZING TIME: 4–5 HOURS

18 CLASSIC ICE CREAMS

STEM GINGER

Very easy to make but with a rather exotic and sophisticated flavour, this ginger ice cream can be matched with a ginger syrup, which is delicious served warm. With its gently warming aftertaste, this recipe is superb served as an end to a dinner party or in cones on a hot day.

INGREDIENTS

280 G/10 OZ JAR STEM GINGER IN SYRUP
2 LARGE EGGS
55 G/2 OZ CASTER SUGAR
300 ML/10 FL OZ DOUBLE CREAM
1 TBSP CLEAR HONEY
2 TBSP HOT WATER

METHOD

● Chop 2 pieces of stem ginger into small pieces, about the size of a pea. ● Separate the eggs in 2 bowls. ● Beat the egg whites until stiff, then beat in the sugar, a spoonful at a time, until the mixture has formed a glossy meringue. ● In a separate bowl, whip the cream until thick but not stiff. ● Break up the egg yolks with a fork and stir them around a little, then add 1 tablespoon of the ginger syrup from the jar. ● Gently fold the meringue into the whipped cream, then stir in the egg-and-syrup mixture and mix gently. ● Finally, stir in the ginger pieces. ● Pour the mixture into a plastic freezerproof container and freeze for at least 6 hours or until solid. ● Remove the ice cream from the freezer and set aside 10 minutes before serving.

PREPARATION TIME: 10 MINUTES
FREEZING TIME: 6 HOURS

To make the syrup (this will make enough for 4 servings): ● Drain the rest of the syrup from the stem ginger. Pour 5 tablespoons of the syrup into a small saucepan. ● Add the honey and hot water and heat gently until the mixture is warm. ● Pour one quarter of the syrup over each serving of ginger ice cream – it has quite a thin texture, but the honey adds a very delicate and delicious taste.

TIP

If you're serving this ice cream as a pudding, try adding a brandy snap or a macaroon to complement the flavours (see pages 114 and 118).

ZABAGLIONE

This rich Italian dessert is usually served at room temperature or slightly chilled. The twist here is that this zabaglione is frozen – making it an excellent finale for a summer dinner. Sprinkle a scattering of crunchy praline (see page 102) on top just before serving.

INGREDIENTS

4 LARGE EGG YOLKS
85 G/3 OZ ICING SUGAR
4 TBSP MARSALA OR SWEET SHERRY
125 ML/4 FL OZ DOUBLE CREAM
PRALINE (SEE PAGE 102), TO SERVE (OPTIONAL)

METHOD

• Put the egg yolks in a large bowl, add the sugar and, using an electric whisk, whisk together for about 3 minutes until very pale, thick and frothy, and a trail of the mixture dropped from the whisk forms a thick 'ribbon' on the surface. • In a separate bowl, whip the Marsala and cream together until thick but not stiff. • Using a spatula, gently fold the egg-and-sugar mixture into the cream and mix carefully but thoroughly. • Divide the mixture among 4 ramekins or small espresso cups, cover the tops with clingfilm and freeze for 2–3 hours or until solid. • Remove the ice cream from the freezer just before serving and scatter the praline over the top, if using.

PREPARATION TIME: 10 MINUTES
FREEZING TIME: 3 HOURS

MOCHA

Chocolate and coffee have a particular affinity, and this ice cream brings out the particular taste of each. It's usually more popular with adults than children and, as it doesn't contain uncooked egg, it is the perfect slightly wicked treat for a pregnant ice-cream lover!

INGREDIENTS

175 G/6 OZ PLAIN CHOCOLATE (AT LEAST 60% COCOA SOLIDS)
2 TBSP FRESHLY MADE ESPRESSO COFFEE OR 1 TSP INSTANT
ESPRESSO POWDER DISSOLVED IN 2 TBSP OF BOILING WATER
300 ML/10 FL OZ DOUBLE CREAM

METHOD

● Break the chocolate into small pieces and put into a heatproof bowl.
● Add the coffee and set the bowl over a saucepan of simmering water, making sure that the base of the bowl does not touch the water. Leave until the chocolate has melted. ● When the chocolate has completely softened, stir briefly with a wooden spoon, then set aside to cool slightly. ● In a separate bowl, whip the cream until thick but not stiff. ● Using a spatula, gently fold the whipped cream into the chocolate-and-coffee mixture. ● Pour the mixture into a plastic freezerproof container and freeze for 4 hours or until solid. ● Remove from the freezer and set aside for 10 minutes before serving.

PREPARATION TIME: 15 MINUTES
FREEZING TIME: 4 HOURS

HONEYCOMB

This custard-based ice cream works well in sugar-waffle cones – the crunch of the waffle complements the sumptuous honey taste perfectly. If you're serving it as part of a meal, a spoonful of real honeycomb on top offers an interesting texture contrast.

INGREDIENTS

4 LARGE EGG YOLKS
50 ML/2 FL OZ CLEAR HONEY
1 TBSP CASTER SUGAR
1 TSP CORNFLOUR
300 ML/10 FL OZ FULL-CREAM MILK
300 ML/10 FL OZ WHIPPING CREAM

METHOD

● Put the egg yolks in a large heatproof bowl. ● Pour the honey into the bowl, add the sugar and cornflour and beat together for 1 minute. ● Pour the milk into a saucepan and bring to the boil then, whisking constantly, pour it slowly over the egg mixture. ● When thoroughly mixed, return the milk-and-egg mixture to the saucepan and warm it gently over a low heat until it forms a thin custard. ● Pour the custard into a bowl and leave to cool. Cover with clingfilm and chill for about 1 hour until cold. ● In a separate bowl, whip the cream until thick but not stiff, then use a spatula to fold it into the custard. Pour the mixture into a plastic freezerproof container and freeze for 1 hour. ● Remove from the freezer and beat thoroughly, then freeze for another 4 hours. ● Remove from the freezer and set aside for 20 minutes before serving.

PREPARATION TIME: 1 HOUR 20 MINUTES
FREEZING TIME: 5 HOURS

HAZELNUT

Nut enthusiasts will particularly appreciate the fine flavour and characteristically slightly rougher texture of this creamy, lightly coffee-coloured ice cream. The sieving process slows the making process slightly but is essential to get the desired result – grainy but not rough.

INGREDIENTS

175 G/6 OZ WHOLE HAZELNUTS
115 G/4 OZ SOFT BROWN SUGAR
300 ML/10 FL OZ FULL-CREAM MILK
300 ML/10 FL OZ DOUBLE CREAM

METHOD

● Preheat the oven to 160°C/335°F/Gas Mark 3. Roast the hazelnuts briefly for 5–10 minutes until lightly browned. Watch closely to make sure they don't burn. ● Remove the hazelnuts from the oven and leave to cool. ● When the hazelnuts have cooled, put them into a food processor or blender and process briefly until finely chopped but not pulverized. ● If using a food processor, transfer the hazelnuts to a blender, then add the sugar and milk and whiz together for a few seconds until a thick, grainy 'cream' forms. ● Transfer the hazelnut mixture to a large bowl, add the cream and stir together thoroughly. ● Pour the mixture through a sieve, pushing through as much of the hazelnut paste as possible with a wooden spoon. ● Scrape the mixture into a plastic freezerproof container and freeze for 3 hours. ● Remove from the freezer, spoon the mixture into a blender and process for a

PREPARATION TIME: 30 MINUTES
FREEZING TIME: 7 HOURS

28

few seconds, then pour the mixture back into the container and freeze for another 4 hours or until solid. ● Remove from the freezer and set aside for 15 minutes before serving.

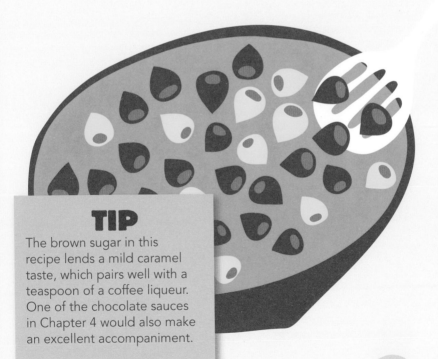

TIP

The brown sugar in this recipe lends a mild caramel taste, which pairs well with a teaspoon of a coffee liqueur. One of the chocolate sauces in Chapter 4 would also make an excellent accompaniment.

PISTACHIO

If you want your pistachio ice cream to come in a nostalgia-inducing pale green, you'll need to add a drop of green food colouring to the recipe – if you don't, it will be a creamy colour, studded with green specks of chopped pistachio.

INGREDIENTS

4 LARGE EGG YOLKS
140 G/5 OZ CASTER SUGAR
300 ML/10 FL OZ FULL-CREAM MILK
175 G/6 OZ WHOLE UNSALTED PISTACHIO NUTS
300 ML/10 FL OZ WHIPPING CREAM
GREEN FOOD COLOURING (OPTIONAL)

METHOD

● Put the yolks into a large bowl. Add the sugar and beat together until thick and creamy. Gradually beat in the milk. ● Pour the mixture into a saucepan and warm it gently over a low heat for a few minutes, stirring constantly, until it thickens to a light custard, the consistency of double cream. Leave to cool. ● While the custard is cooling, chop the pistachios (you can use a blender or food processor, but you may find it easier to chop them by hand on a wooden board with a sharp knife). ● In a separate bowl, whip the cream until thick but not stiff. ● Using a spatula, gently fold the cream into the cooled custard, then mix in the pistachio pieces and food colouring, if using. (Keep the colouring subtle; the end effect should be delicately pastel, not Hammer Horror!) ● Pour the mixture into a plastic freezerproof container and freeze for

PREPARATION TIME: 30 MINUTES
FREEZING TIME: 7 HOURS

3 hours. ● Remove from the freezer, empty the mixture into a bowl and whisk thoroughly. ● Pour the mixture back into the container and freeze for at least 4 hours or until solid. ● Remove from the freezer and set aside for 20 minutes before serving.

TIP

Buy whole pistachios if you can. Chop them just before adding to the ice cream as this will enhance the flavour – the more coarsely they are chopped, the more pronounced the pistachio 'hit'.

BROWN BREAD

Today, brown-bread ice cream is treated as something of a curiosity but, in fact, this is one of the oldest of ice cream recipes, recorded and relished in early Victorian times. Although it's less well-known today, everyone should try it at least once.

INGREDIENTS

3 THICK SLICES GOOD-QUALITY WHOLEMEAL BREAD
300 ML/10 FL OZ DOUBLE CREAM
150 ML/5 FL OZ SINGLE CREAM
115 G/4 OZ LIGHT BROWN SUGAR
2 LARGE EGGS
1 TBSP RUM (OPTIONAL)

METHOD

● Preheat the oven to 190°C/375°F/Gas Mark 5. Rub the bread lightly to make large crumbs, or blitz it briefly in a blender or food processor. Discard any pieces of crust that won't 'crumb' easily. ● Put the breadcrumbs on a baking tray and toast in the oven for 5–10 minutes, or until they are crisp but not crunchy. ● Pour both creams into a large bowl. Add the sugar and whip together until thick but not stiff. ● Separate the eggs into 2 bowls. Beat the egg yolks and rum, if using, together with a fork. ● Using a spatula, gently fold the egg-yolk mixture into the sweetened cream, then fold in the cooled breadcrumbs. ● Beat the egg whites until stiff, then fold them into the mixture with a spatula. ● Pour the mixture into a plastic freezerproof container and freeze for at least 4 hours or until solid. ● Remove from the freezer and set aside for 10 minutes before serving.

PREPARATION TIME: 30 MINUTES
FREEZING TIME: 4–5 HOURS

CHESTNUT

This rich and very sweet chestnut parfait can be served in individual dishes or turned out of small dariole moulds. It's quick and easy because the sweetened chestnut purée comes ready prepared in a can, and yet it tastes very distinctive.

INGREDIENTS

115 G/4 OZ CANNED SWEETENED CHESTNUT PURÉE
6 TBSP COLD WATER
225 G/8 OZ GRANULATED SUGAR
4 LARGE EGGS
225 ML/8 FL OZ WHIPPING CREAM

METHOD

● Put the chestnut purée into a bowl and mash with a fork until smooth.
● Place the water in a saucepan, add the sugar, stir, then bring to the boil and boil without stirring until the sugar has dissolved. When it starts to colour, remove from the heat. ● Separate the eggs, putting the egg yolks into one bowl and 2 of the whites into another. Beat the egg yolks until thick and pale, then gradually beat in the hot syrup. ● When the syrup has been added, carry on beating until the mixture is light and foamy. Beat in the chestnut purée, a little at a time. ● Beat the egg whites until soft peaks form. ● Using a spatula, fold the cream and egg whites into the chestnut mixture. ● Pour the mixture into 4 large ramekins or small dariole moulds, or 6 espresso cups, and freeze for 3 hours. ● Remove from the freezer 10 minutes before serving. To turn out the moulds, dip in hot water, then invert on a plate.

PREPARATION TIME: 30 MINUTES
FREEZING TIME: 3 HOURS

   CLASSIC ICE CREAMS

DULCE DE LECHE

This dulce de leche ice cream is one of the easiest recipes of all and a favourite with most children. The dulce de leche gives this ice cream an irresistibly rich caramel flavour – there may not be anything sophisticated about it, but you'll find that it's extremely popular.

INGREDIENTS

2 LARGE EGGS
55 G/2 OZ CASTER SUGAR
300 ML/10 FL OZ DOUBLE CREAM
1 400 G/160 OZ JAR DULCE DE LECHE CARAMEL OR 1 400 G/14 OZ CAN CONDENSED MILK
(IF YOU ARE MAKING YOUR OWN DULCE DE LECHE, PIERCE THE TOP OF THE CAN OF CONDENSED MILK AND PUT IN A PAN. POUR IN ENOUGH SIMMERING WATER TO COME HALFWAY UP THE SIDE OF THE CAN, THEN BRING TO THE BOIL AND BOIL FOR 3 HOURS, TOPPING UP THE WATER EVERY SO OFTEN. LEAVE TO COOL. WHEN YOU OPEN THE CAN, YOU WILL FIND THE MILK HAS TURNED TO SOFT CARAMEL.)
1 TSP LEMON JUICE

METHOD

● Separate the eggs into 2 bowls. ● Beat the egg whites until stiff, then beat in the sugar, a spoonful at a time, until the mixture has formed a glossy meringue. ● In a separate bowl, whip the cream until thick but not stiff. ● Break up the egg yolks with a fork and stir them around a little. Add 5 tablespoons of the dulce de leche and beat together until thoroughly mixed. Add the lemon juice and beat it into the mixture. ● Using a spatula, gently fold the whipped cream gently into the meringue. When it is almost incorporated, gradually fold in

PREPARATION TIME: 10 MINUTES
FREEZING TIME: 6 HOURS

the caramel-and-egg yolk mixture. ● When the ice cream is mixed, swirl through 2 more tablespoons of the dulce de leche, shaking small dollops of caramel from the spoon. This will give your finished ice cream pockets of luscious pure caramel. ● Pour the ice cream mixture into a plastic freezerproof container and freeze for at least 6 hours or until solid. ● Remove the ice cream from the freezer and set aside for 10 minutes before serving.

ROCKY ROAD

A rich confection of chocolate ice cream studded with more chocolate, marshmallow and nuts. Opinion is divided as to which nuts taste best. This version uses pecans, but almonds are the most commonly found. Whichever you choose, serve this ice in small scoops – it's very rich!

INGREDIENTS

55 G/2 OZ PECAN NUTS
175 G/6 OZ PLAIN CHOCOLATE
ALMOND EXTRACT, TO TASTE (OPTIONAL)
300 ML/10 FL OZ DOUBLE CREAM
55 G/2 OZ MINIATURE MARSHMALLOWS, OR THE REGULAR SIZE CHOPPED INTO HAZELNUT-SIZED PIECES
55 G/2 OZ MILK CHOCOLATE CHIPS

METHOD

● Preheat the oven to 160°C/325°F/Gas Mark 3. Spread the pecan nuts out on a baking tray and toast them for 5–10 minutes until lightly browned. Watch them carefully to make sure they don't burn. Leave to cool, then chop into medium-sized pieces. ● Break the chocolate into small pieces and put into a heatproof bowl set over a saucepan of simmering water. Add 2–3 drops of the almond extract, if using (it adds a subtle flavour to the end result), and leave until the chocolate has melted. ● Meanwhile, in a separate bowl, whip the cream until thick but not stiff. ● Remove the chocolate from the heat, leave to cool slightly, then beat it into the cream. ● When the chocolate and cream are thoroughly mixed, add the pecans, marshmallows and the

PREPARATION TIME: 30 MINUTES
FREEZING TIME: 4 HOURS

milk chocolate chips and mix them through the ice cream. ● Pour the mixture into a plastic freezerproof container and freeze for 4 hours or until solid. ● Remove the ice cream from the freezer and set aside for 10 minutes before serving.

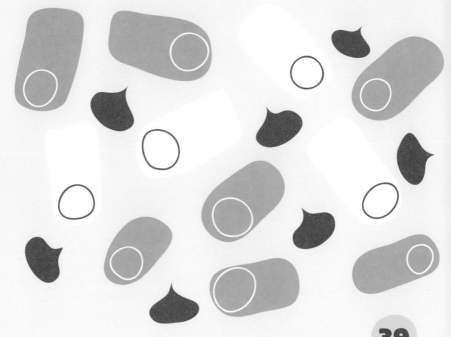

CLASSIC LEMON

Although lemon is more often seen as a sorbet flavour in contemporary ice-cream parlours, it makes a delectable creamy ice. Try this one once, and you won't look back – it's both light and rich, with a citrus tang that cuts the creaminess to great effect.

INGREDIENTS

3 UNWAXED LEMONS
115 G/4 OZ ICING SUGAR
300 ML/10 FL OZ DOUBLE CREAM

METHOD

● Put a couple of ice cubes into a glass of water and set aside.
● Zest the lemons, using either a purpose-made lemon zester or the fine side of an ordinary grater into a bowl. Squeeze 2 of the lemons and add the juice to the zest. ● Add the sugar and stir until it has dissolved. ● In a separate bowl, whip the cream with 2 tablespoons of the chilled water until thick but not stiff. ● Whisk the sugar and lemon mixture into the cream until it is thoroughly combined. ● Pour the mixture into a plastic freezerproof container and freeze for at least 4 hours or until solid. ● Remove the ice cream from the freezer and set aside for 15 minutes before serving.

PREPARATION TIME: 10 MINUTES
FREEZING TIME: 4 HOURS

40   CLASSIC ICE CREAMS

PRALINE

This is a semifreddo, which literally means 'half-frozen'. It is softer in texture than most ice creams – a result achieved with the high proportion of egg yolks in the recipe. It is easiest made in a narrow, tall container, such as a loaf tin lined with clingfilm.

INGREDIENTS

1 LARGE EGG AND 4 LARGE EGG YOLKS
85 G/3 OZ SOFT BROWN SUGAR
350 ML/12 FL OZ DOUBLE CREAM
115 G/4 OZ PRALINE (SEE PAGES 102–3)

METHOD

● Line the container you plan to use with clingfilm, folding it into the corners and leaving surplus hanging over the edges. ● Put the whole egg and the egg yolks into a large bowl. ● Add the sugar and set the bowl over a saucepan of hot but not boiling water, making sure the base of the bowl is not touching the water. Using an electric whisk, beat the mixture until very light and pale, then remove the bowl from the saucepan and set aside. ● In a separate bowl, whip the cream until thick but not stiff. ● Using a spatula, gently fold the egg-and-sugar mixture into the whipped cream. ● Gently fold in 85 g/3 oz of the praline. ● Pour the mixture into the prepared container and freeze for 3 hours. Unlike some ice creams, this recipe can be served straight from the freezer – simply turn the semifreddo out of its container, peel off the clingfilm and scatter the remaining praline over the top to serve.

PREPARATION TIME: 15 MINUTES
FREEZING TIME: 3 HOURS

TIP

Consider passing the ice cream round the table with a small jug of maple syrup to pour over it – the maple flavour complements the nutty praline brilliantly.

CHAPTER 2
FRESH FRUIT
FLAVOURS

Chocolate may be luscious and coffee sophisticated, but for a real summer taste, there's nothing to beat fresh fruit ices – and one of the pleasures of using fruit is that you can always make something absolutely appropriate to the season. There's a wide range here, from a traditional raspberry ice cream and fruit lollies you can happily offer small children (no additives, no artificial colourings), to a few frozen drinks, which are not strictly scoopable, perhaps, but certainly icy and sumptuous enough to have earned their inclusion.

RASPBERRY

One of the best fruit flavours of all when frozen, raspberry makes a classic scooping ice – great in cones on a hot day. This ice cream has quite a high egg content but is comparatively low in cream, allowing the raspberry taste to come through.

INGREDIENTS

250 G/9 OZ FRESH RASPBERRIES
3 LARGE EGGS
115 G/4 OZ CASTER SUGAR
150 ML/5 FL OZ DOUBLE CREAM

METHOD

● Put the raspberries into a blender and blitz for a few 5-second bursts until a thick purée forms. Push it through a sieve into a bowl, rubbing as much of the fruit through with a wooden spoon as you can. Discard the pips left in the sieve. ● Separate the eggs into 2 large bowls. Beat the egg whites until soft peaks form, then beat in half of the sugar, a spoonful at a time, until the mixture is a glossy meringue. ● Add the rest of the sugar to the egg yolks and beat together until thick and pale and when the beaters are lifted the mixture leaves a ribbon-like trail on the surface. ● In a separate bowl, whip the cream until thick but not stiff. ● Using a spatula, carefully fold the raspberry purée into the egg-yolk mixture, then fold it into the meringue. ● Gently fold in the whipped cream. ● Pour the mixture into a plastic freezerproof container and freeze for at least 6 hours. ● Remove the ice cream from the freezer and set aside for 15 minutes before serving.

PREPARATION TIME: 15 MINUTES
FREEZING TIME: 6 HOURS

FRESH PEACH

This fresh-peach ice-cream recipe will adapt well to other stone fruit, too – plum is especially delicious – provided that you use the correct balance of fruit purée to the other ingredients.

INGREDIENTS

4 RIPE PEACHES
55 G/2 OZ ICING SUGAR
4 LARGE EGG YOLKS
1 LEMON
2 TSP POWDERED GELATINE
300 ML/10 FL OZ DOUBLE CREAM

METHOD

● Put the peaches into a bowl of boiling water and leave for 1 minute, then remove and skin (the boiling water makes it easier to peel off the skins). Cut the peaches in half, remove the stones and cut the flesh into chunks. ● Put the peach flesh into a blender, add the sugar and blitz until a thick purée forms. Transfer to a bowl. ● Mix the egg yolks into the peaches with a fork. ● Squeeze the lemon and put 3 tablespoons of the juice into a small heatproof bowl. Sprinkle over the gelatine and set the bowl over a saucepan of hot water. Stir the mixture over a low heat, then remove the bowl from the saucepan and set aside. ● Set the bowl of peach purée over the saucepan of simmering water and stir until it thickens slightly, then add the dissolved gelatine and mix

PREPARATION TIME: 45 MINUTES
FREEZING TIME: 7 HOURS

48

together. Remove from the heat and leave to cool. ● In a separate bowl, whip the cream until thick but not stiff. ● Using a spatula, gently fold the whipped cream into the cooled purée, then pour the mixture into a freezerproof container and freeze for 3 hours. ● Remove from the freezer and whisk thoroughly with an electric whisk, then return to the freezer for at least another 4 hours. ● Remove from the freezer 20 minutes before serving.

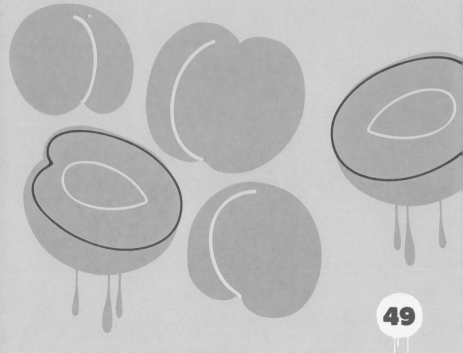

GRAPEFRUIT

This delicate syrup-based sorbet is one strictly for grown-ups as it contains vodka. It isn't the most appropriate sorbet to be scooped into cones; it works best served in bowls and savoured with a small spoon, perhaps with an almond tuile (see pages 108–9) on the side.

INGREDIENTS

225 G/8 OZ GRANULATED SUGAR
1.7 LITRES/3 PINTS COLD WATER
3 LARGE JUICY GRAPEFRUIT
1 LARGE EGG WHITE
90 ML/3 FL OZ VODKA

METHOD

● Put the sugar and water into a saucepan and place over a low heat, stirring, until the sugar has dissolved. Bring the mixture just to boiling point and boil for 5 minutes without stirring. Remove from the heat and leave to cool. ● Squeeze the grapefruit, reserving the juice in a jug and removing any pips. ● Beat the egg white in a large bowl until stiff. ● When the sugar syrup is completely cold, pour in the grapefruit juice and vodka and mix well. If you want a completely smooth sorbet strain the grapefruit juice through a sieve, but if you like one containing little pieces of fruit pulp, then add it as it is. ● Using a metal spoon, stir the beaten egg white into the grapefruit syrup and mix well. ● Pour the mixture into a plastic freezerproof container and freeze for 3 hours. ● Remove the sorbet from the freezer, empty it into a bowl and whisk

PREPARATION TIME: 30 MINUTES
FREEZING TIME: 7 HOURS

well. Return to the container and freeze for another 4 hours or until it is completely set. ● Remove the sorbet from the freezer and set aside for 5 minutes before serving. (Note that using vodka in the recipe means that this sorbet will remain softer than others.)

TIP

Use pink grapefruit if you can find them – the resulting sorbet will freeze to a delectable pale shell pink.

FRUIT LOLLIES

If you have children you'll already have made those lollies that are simply plain juice poured into moulds and frozen. These fresh-fruit lollies are based on a sugar syrup, which makes them a little more luscious and a bit less 'icy' than pure frozen juice.

INGREDIENTS

450 G/1 LB RIPE STRAWBERRIES
1 LEMON
140 G/5 OZ CASTER SUGAR
250 ML/9 FL OZ COLD WATER

METHOD

● Hull the strawberries, put them in a blender and blitz until a thick, seedy purée forms. ● Squeeze the lemon and add the juice to the purée, stirring it thoroughly. ● Put the sugar and water in a saucepan and place over a low heat, stirring, until the sugar has dissolved. Bring the mixture to the boil and boil for 5 minutes without stirring. Remove the syrup from the heat and leave to cool. ● When the sugar syrup is cold, rub the purée through a sieve into the syrup, rubbing as much of the fruit through with a wooden spoon as you can. ● Decant the mixture into your chosen moulds and place on a level surface in the freezer. ● Freeze for 3–4 hours. ● Remove the lollies from the freezer and eat straight away.

PREPARATION TIME: 1 HOUR
FREEZING TIME: 3–4 HOURS

APPLE & BERRY

An apple ice cream with a blackberry sauce is the taste of autumn in a cone. The combination is just as good a marriage for ice cream as it is in an autumnal pie. This recipe is quite labour-intensive, but the results are well worth the effort.

INGREDIENTS

280 G/10 OZ EATING APPLES
(SUCH AS COX, BRAEBURN OR DISCOVERY)
1 TBSP COLD WATER
6 LARGE EGG YOLKS
115 G/4 OZ CASTER SUGAR
300 ML/10 FL OZ DOUBLE CREAM
50 ML/2 FL OZ FULL-CREAM MILK

FOR THE BLACKBERRY SAUCE:
140 G/5 OZ BLACKBERRIES
25 G/1 OZ CASTER SUGAR

METHOD

● Peel the apples and cut into chunks. Put them in a saucepan with the water and cook over a low heat until stewed. Remove from the heat and leave to cool. ● When the apple has cooled, blitz it in a blender until smooth. Transfer to a bowl and leave to chill. ● Put the egg yolks and sugar in a large bowl and, using an electric whisk, beat until the mixture is thick and pale. ● Pour the cream and milk into a saucepan and place over a low heat until almost boiling. ● Remove from the heat and pour over the egg-yolk mixture, beating constantly. Return to

PREPARATION TIME: 1 HOUR 30 MINUTES
FREEZING TIME: 7 HOURS

54 FRESH FRUIT FLAVOURS

the pan and heat gently, stirring all the time, until the mixture thickens to a thin custard the consistency of double cream. Set the custard aside to cool. ● When it is cold, fold in the apple purée. ● Pour into a plastic freezerproof container and freeze for 2 hours. ● Remove from the freezer and whisk thoroughly. Return to the freezer and freeze for another 2 hours, then remove and beat again. ● Return to the freezer for another 3 hours or until solid. ● Remove the ice cream from the freezer and set aside for 15 minutes before serving.

To make the blackberry sauce: ● Put the blackberries and sugar in a bowl and mix together. ● Transfer them to a blender and blitz for 10 seconds until thoroughly broken down. ● Sieve the purée into a small jug and serve with the ice cream.

PINEAPPLE

The tropical quality in the flavour of the grilled pineapple makes this ice cream especially luxurious. If you use the Malibu a faint flavour of coconut will complement the pineapple. It takes a little time to make, but it's well worth trying for the depth of taste.

INGREDIENTS

1 SMALL RIPE PINEAPPLE
85 G/3 OZ SOFT BROWN SUGAR
2 LARGE EGGS
300 ML/10 FL OZ DOUBLE CREAM
1 TBSP MALIBU LIQUEUR (OPTIONAL)

METHOD

● Preheat the grill and line the grill pan with foil. ● Peel and core the pineapple and cut the fruit into slices about 1 cm/½ in thick, then cut each slice into quarters. ● Lay the pineapple pieces on the foil-lined grill pan and scatter 25 g/1 oz of the sugar over the top. ● Grill the pineapple until the fruit is hot and the sugar is caramelizing slightly but not burnt. ● Weigh out 140 g/5 oz of the caramelized fruit (set the rest aside for an accompaniment to the finished ice cream), put it into a blender and blitz to a purée. ● Pour the purée into a bowl and leave to chill. ● Separate the eggs into 2 bowls. Beat the egg whites until stiff, then beat in the remaining sugar, a spoonful at a time, until the mixture has formed a shiny, slightly golden meringue. ● In a separate bowl, whip the cream until thick but not stiff. ● Add the egg yolks to

PREPARATION TIME: 30 MINUTES
FREEZING TIME: 6 HOURS

the pineapple purée and mix together with a fork. Stir in the Malibu, if using. ● Using a spatula, gently fold the cream into the meringue, then fold in the pineapple purée until it is well combined. ● Pour the mixture into a plastic freezerproof container and freeze for 6 hours or overnight until solid. ● Remove the ice cream from the freezer and set aside for 15 minutes before serving. Serve with the reserved caramelized pineapple if you like.

BANANA

Banana ice cream tends to inspire extreme reactions – that is, people either love it or hate it. It's milder in flavour than many of the other fruit ices, but it tends to be popular with children, especially if it's served up alongside a butterscotch sauce (see page 103).

INGREDIENTS

1 LEMON
3 LARGE RIPE BANANAS, OR 4 SMALLER ONES
150 ML/5 FL OZ FULL FAT GREEK YOGURT
150 ML/5 FL OZ DOUBLE CREAM
2 LARGE EGG WHITES
55 G/2 OZ SOFT BROWN SUGAR

METHOD

• Squeeze the lemon and put 2 tablespoons of the juice into a bowl. Peel and slice the bananas and add them to the juice. • Vigorously mash the bananas, then beat them with an electric whisk until smooth. Fold in the Greek yogurt. • In a separate bowl, whip the cream until thick but not stiff. • Using a spatula, gently fold the whipped cream into the banana mixture, then transfer to a plastic freezerproof container and freeze for 2 hours. • While the banana cream is freezing, put the egg whites in a bowl and beat until stiff, then beat in the sugar, a spoonful at a time, until the mixture has formed a glossy meringue. • Remove the banana cream from the freezer, empty it into a large bowl and beat it with an electric whisk. • Fold the meringue into the frozen mixture

PREPARATION TIME: 15 MINUTES
FREEZING TIME: 6 HOURS

and mix until smooth. ● Pour the mixture back into the container and freeze for another 3–4 hours or until solid. ● Remove the ice cream from the freezer and set aside for 10 minutes before serving.

LEMON CURD

If you ever feel nostalgic for the homely childhood taste of a lemon meringue pie, you'll find all the same flavours here in a sharp, citrus ice scattered with sweet little fragments of meringue.

INGREDIENTS

300 ML/10 FL OZ WHIPPING CREAM
125 ML/4 FL OZ GREEK YOGURT
1 LEMON
115 G/4 OZ LEMON CURD, PREFERABLY ORGANIC
3 LARGE MERINGUES (SEE PAGES 122–23)

METHOD

● Put the cream into a large bowl and whip until thick but not stiff. Using a spatula, fold in the yogurt. ● Zest the lemon into a bowl, either using a purpose-made lemon zester or the fine side of an ordinary grater. Squeeze the lemon and mix with the zest in the bowl. ● Add the lemon curd to the lemon juice mixture and mix with a fork until combined. ● Gently fold the lemon mixture into the cream and yogurt. ● Break the meringues into pieces (keep a few large ones so that their texture will be noticeable) and fold them into the cream mixture. ● Pour the mixture into a plastic freezerproof container and freeze for 4–6 hours or until solid. ● Remove the ice cream from the freezer just before serving.

PREPARATION TIME: 10 MINUTES
FREEZING TIME: 6 HOURS

LEMON ICE

We may as well be clear from the outset – strictly speaking, this is something between a sorbet and a granita and is drunk rather than scooped. In Spain it's available from every café during the hot weather. This recipe will make two tall glasses.

INGREDIENTS

6 LEMONS
115 G/4 OZ CASTER SUGAR
2 TRAYS OF ICE CUBES

METHOD

● Squeeze the lemons and pour the juice into a bowl, removing any pips. ● Add the sugar and stir thoroughly, then leave to stand for 30 minutes until the sugar has dissolved. ● Empty the ice cubes into a blender, pour in the lemon-juice mixture and blend on a high speed until the mixture is part small ice crystals and part liquid. ● Pour into 2 tall glasses, distributing the ice and liquid evenly between them, and serve.

Variation
To make coffee granizado, make 600 ml/1 pint of strong black coffee, add the sugar and stir until the sugar has dissolved. Chill the coffee in the refrigerator for 2 hours. When it's cold, proceed as above.

PREPARATION TIME: 35 MINUTES
NO FREEZING TIME, BUT YOU NEED
READYMADE ICE

BERRY RIPPLE

This strawberry ripple ice cream is just as delicious as a raspberry ripple. The base is taken from the classic vanilla recipe on pages 12–13 – the ripple is simply made by puréeing strawberries and sugar together. The vinegar offsets the strawberry taste really well.

INGREDIENTS

175 G/6 OZ RIPE STRAWBERRIES
55 G/2 OZ ICING SUGAR
1 TSP BALSAMIC VINEGAR (OPTIONAL)
2 LARGE EGGS
55 G/2 OZ CASTER SUGAR
300 ML/10 FL OZ DOUBLE CREAM
1 TSP VANILLA EXTRACT

METHOD

● Hull the strawberries, put them in a large bowl and sprinkle them with the icing sugar and balsamic vinegar, if using. ● Transfer the strawberry mixture to a blender and blitz briefly until reduced to a purée. Rub the purée through a sieve into a bowl so you are left with a thick sauce. ● Put the sauce into a plastic freezerproof container and freeze. ● Separate the eggs into 2 bowls. Beat the egg whites until stiff, then beat in the remaining sugar, a spoonful at a time, until the mixture has formed a glossy meringue. ● In a separate bowl, whip the cream until thick but not stiff. ● Beat the egg yolks with a fork, then mix in the vanilla extract. ● Using a spatula, gently fold the cream into the meringue, then mix in the egg yolks. ● Remove the strawberry

PREPARATION TIME: 1 HOUR
FREEZING TIME: 6 HOURS

64 FRESH FRUIT FLAVOURS

sauce from the freezer ● Pour a third of the vanilla ice cream into another plastic freezerproof container, then spoon in a thin layer of strawberry sauce, using about half of it. Add another third of the ice cream, then add the rest of the strawberry sauce in another layer. Pour the remainder of the ice cream on top. ● Create the ripples by running a skewer in an 'S'-shape through the ice cream. This will leave trails of strawberry without it mixing in too much.● Freeze the mixture for 5–6 hours or until firm. ● Remove the ice cream from the freezer and set aside for 15 minutes before serving.

RUBY PARFAIT

The beautiful ruby red of blood-orange juice gives this frozen parfait an exotic air. Lusciously rich, it's a good dessert for a dinner party – rich, delicious and readily prepared in advance. Blood-orange parfait is delicious served with tiny macaroons (see pages 118–19).

INGREDIENTS

450 ML/16 FL OZ BLOOD-ORANGE JUICE
4 LARGE EGG YOLKS
55 G/2 OZ GOLDEN CASTER SUGAR
30 ML/1 FL OZ LIQUID GLUCOSE
1 TBSP BRANDY OR COINTREAU (OPTIONAL)
200 ML/7 FL OZ DOUBLE CREAM

METHOD

● Pour the orange juice into a saucepan, place over a low heat and bring to the boil. Turn the heat down as low as possible and simmer the juice for 15 minutes until it has reduced by about half. Remove the pan from the heat and leave to cool. ● Put the egg yolks in a heatproof bowl and add the cooled orange juice, the sugar, the liquid glucose and the brandy, if using. ● Set the bowl over a saucepan of simmering water and, using an electric whisk, beat the mixture for 5–10 minutes until thick and creamy. ● Remove the bowl from the heat and beat for another 5 minutes as it cools, then set aside. ● In a separate bowl, whip the cream until thick but not stiff. ● Using a spatula, gently fold the orange juice mixture into the whipped cream, mixing it lightly but

PREPARATION TIME: 45 MINUTES
FREEZING TIME: 5-6 HOURS

thoroughly. ● Pour the mixture into a plastic freezerproof container and freeze for 5–6 hours or until solid. ● Remove the parfait from the freezer 5 minutes before serving.

TIP

Liquid glucose can be bought at the chemist. If you can't find fresh ruby oranges, buy a carton of the juice from the supermarket.

MIXED BERRY

Use the frozen berry mixes found in the supermarket freezer compartments to make this all year round. The ideal mix would be raspberries, strawberries and blueberries – the rich flavours of each meld together to make a vivid, deeply flavoured ice cream.

INGREDIENTS

350 G/12 OZ MIXTURE OF FRESH
OR FROZEN (THAWED) SUMMER BERRIES
115 G/4 OZ ICING SUGAR
2 LARGE EGGS
300 ML/10 FL OZ DOUBLE CREAM

METHOD

● Put the berries and half the sugar into a blender and blitz briefly until a rich, dark purée forms. ● Divide the purée in half. Rub one half through a sieve into a jug to make a coulis and leave to chill. Put the other half in a bowl and set aside. ● Separate the eggs into 2 large bowls. Beat the egg whites until stiff, then beat in the remaining sugar, a spoonful at a time, until the mixture has formed a meringue. ● In a separate bowl, whip the cream until thick but not stiff. ● Beat the egg yolks with a fork, add the reserved fruit purée and mix. ● Fold the cream into the meringue, then mix in the fruit and egg-yolk mixture. ● Pour the mixture into a plastic freezerproof container and freeze for 5–6 hours or until solid. ● Remove from the freezer and set aside for 15 minutes before serving. ● Serve with the chilled coulis.

PREPARATION TIME: 45 MINUTES
FREEZING TIME: 5–6 HOURS

BERRY SOUFFLÉ

The luscious texture of this frozen soufflé comes from the cooking method – unlike most of the other ices, this one is based on a meringue made by whipping a hot sugar syrup into beaten egg whites. The result is an airy and rich texture – well worth the effort.

INGREDIENTS

450 G/1 LB BLACKCURRANTS
350 G/12 OZ CASTER SUGAR
125 ML/4 FL OZ COLD WATER, PLUS 3 TBSP
4 LARGE EGGS WHITES
300 ML/10 FL OZ DOUBLE CREAM

METHOD

● Put the blackcurrants in a saucepan with 115 g/4 oz of the sugar and the 3 tablespoons of water. Place over a low heat and simmer for 5 minutes until the fruit has collapsed. ● Transfer to a blender and whiz for a few seconds. Rub the berries through a sieve into a bowl, rubbing as much of the fruit through with a wooden spoon as you can. Leave to cool. ● Put the remaining sugar in a saucepan with the remaining water, place over a low heat and stir until the sugar has dissolved. Bring the mixture to the boil and boil, without stirring, until the mixture reaches 120°C/248°F on a sugar thermometer. If you do not have a sugar thermometer, the syrup is ready when a small quantity is dropped into cold water and forms a hard ball. ● While the syrup is boiling, put the egg whites into a large bowl and beat until soft peaks form. ● As

PREPARATION TIME: 1 HOUR
FREEZING TIME: 4–5 HOURS

soon as the syrup reaches the 'hard ball' stage, pour it slowly onto the egg whites, whisking constantly as you do so. By the time you have added the last of the syrup, the mixture will have formed a very shiny, dense meringue. Leave to chill. ● In a separate bowl, whip the cream until thick but not stiff. ● Using a spatula, fold the blackcurrant purée into the whipped cream, then fold in the meringue. ● Pour the mixture into a plastic freezerproof container or a soufflé dish and freeze for at least 4 hours or until solid. ● Remove the soufflé from the freezer just before serving.

TIP

You can make a redcurrant or blackberry souffle in exactly the same way. Simply replace the blackcurrants with an equal weight of either fruit.

CHAPTER 3
SORBETS &
UNUSUAL ICES

These recipes are less cream-focused than the typical ice, although some do include modest amounts of milk or cream. Sorbets, sherbets and even kulfi all offer possible alternatives if your idea of an iced treat isn't heavy on cream. And if you're actually dairy-intolerant there is a generous range of recipes that you can try, from an abstemious (but still delicious) chocolate sorbet to a wonderfully sharp lime-and-ginger refresher – a sherbet lift for a hot day.

MANGO KULFI

Kulfi is Indian ice cream – lush and delicious, usually warmly redolent of cardamom and other spices. It has a very particular flavour and is most commonly found in mango or pistachio varieties. You can make the kulfi in either a large container or small metal dariole moulds.

INGREDIENTS

1 TBSP CORNFLOUR
1 TBSP COLD WATER
600 ML/1 PINT EVAPORATED MILK
175 G/6 OZ CASTER SUGAR
1 LARGE RIPE MANGO
150 ML/5 FL OZ SINGLE CREAM
½ TSP GROUND CARDAMOM

METHOD

● Put the cornflour and water into a cup and mix thoroughly. ● Pour the evaporated milk into a saucepan and bring to the boil over a medium heat. When it boils, stir in the cornflour mixture. Continue to stir as the milk thickens; within a couple of minutes it should have thickened to a custard. Quickly add the sugar, stirring, until the sugar has dissolved. Remove from the heat and set aside. ● Peel the mango and cut the flesh into small chunks. ● Put the fruit into a blender and whiz briefly in 5-second bursts until a purée forms. ● Pour the cream into the evaporated milk mixture and stir to combine. Stir in the mango and ground cardamom and mix thoroughly. ● Transfer the mixture to a plastic freezerproof container and freeze for 1½ hours. ● Remove the

PREPARATION TIME: 15 MINUTES
FREEZING TIME: 7 HOURS 30 MINUTES

kulfi from the freezer and beat well. Return to the freezer and freeze for another hour, then repeat the process. ● After the second beating you can transfer it to 6 dariole moulds if you are making individual kulfis, then freeze for another 5 hours or overnight. ● Remove the kulfi from the freezer 5 minutes before serving. Either scoop from the large container, or dip the dariole moulds briefly in hot water and turn them out onto serving plates.

TIP

You can freeze the kulfi in a plastic freezer container as usual, or you can make individual portions in small metal dariole moulds. You will need 6 of the latter.

CAFÉ GRANITA

A granita is a flavourful mass of tiny ice crystals – the crystals that you beat out of a sorbet are allowed to form without interruption in a granita, making it one of the easiest frozen treats of all to make.

INGREDIENTS

2 ESPRESSO CUPFULS OF FRESHLY MADE ESPRESSO COFFEE
115 G/4 OZ CASTER SUGAR
300 ML/10 FL OZ BOILING WATER

METHOD

● Put the coffee and sugar into a heatproof bowl. ● Pour in the boiling water and stir until the sugar has dissolved, then leave to cool. ● When the liquid is cold, pour it into a shallow freezerproof tray and place in the freezer. ● Leave until frozen solid (this usually takes about 4 hours), then turn out of the container, break into large chunks and blitz in a blender for just a few seconds. Return to the container and freeze again (usually another 4 hours). ● When you are ready to serve, remove from the freezer and scrape it into pieces with a fork. For each serving, fill a small bowl with a heap of icy shards.

PREPARATION TIME: 30 MINUTES
FREEZING TIME: 8 HOURS

LEMON CRUNCH

A serving of crunchy lemon ice makes a light treat. Don't be tempted to add more sugar to this granita – you want the sharpness of the lemon to come through alongside the sweetness.

INGREDIENTS

3 JUICY LEMONS
115 G/4 OZ CASTER SUGAR
600 ML/1 PINT COLD WATER

METHOD

● Squeeze the lemons and put the juice into a small jug. ● Put the sugar and water into a saucepan and place over a low heat, stirring, until the sugar has dissolved. ● Increase the heat slightly, bring the syrup to the boil and boil for 5 minutes. ● Add the lemon juice to the syrup and leave to cool. ● When the syrup is cold, pour into a shallow freezerproof container and freeze until solid. ● Remove it from the freezer, break into large chunks and blitz in a blender for just a few seconds, then return to the container and freeze for 4 hours. ● When you are ready to serve the granita, remove it from the freezer and scrape it into pieces with a fork.

PREPARATION TIME: 45 MINUTES
FREEZING TIME: 8 HOURS

MARMALADE

Although this ice cream features cream, the richness of the end effect is quite sharply cut by the inclusion of yogurt. The marmalade flavour is surprising, too – it's slightly orangey and candied, and for the first mouthful your guests may not be quite able to place it.

INGREDIENTS

280 G/10 OZ THICK-CUT SEVILLE MARMALADE
150 ML/5 FL OZ GREEK YOGURT
40 G/1½ OZ ICING SUGAR
1 LEMON
1 TSP ORANGE FLOWER WATER (OPTIONAL)
450 ML/15 FL OZ WHIPPING CREAM

METHOD

● Put the marmalade into a large bowl, add the yogurt and sugar and, using an electric whisk, beat together until smooth. ● Squeeze the lemon and add 1 tablespoon of the juice to the marmalade mixture, along with the orange-flower water, if using, then stir together. ● In a separate bowl, whip the cream until it holds its shape. ● Using a spatula, gently fold the cream into the marmalade-and-yogurt mixture, mixing gently but thoroughly until it is combined. ● Pour the mixture into a plastic freezerproof container and freeze for 2 hours. ● Remove from the freezer and mix thoroughly, then return to the freezer and freeze for at least 5 hours. ● Remove the ice cream from the freezer and set aside for 10 minutes before serving.

PREPARATION TIME: 10 MINUTES
FREEZING TIME: 7 HOURS

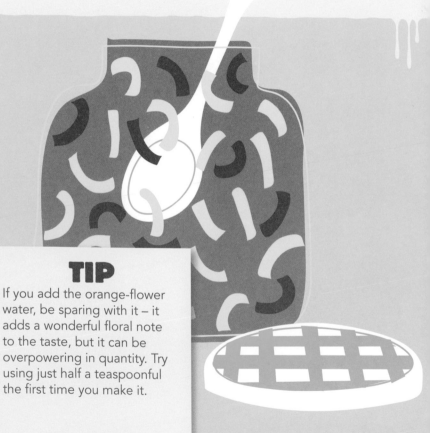

TIP

If you add the orange-flower water, be sparing with it – it adds a wonderful floral note to the taste, but it can be overpowering in quantity. Try using just half a teaspoonful the first time you make it.

PAPAYA & LIME

Just like pineapple and ginger, papaya paired with lime offers a distinctly tropical sorbet. This recipe is also a good way of using papayas that are less than perfectly ripe while still allowing you to benefit from their particular flavour.

INGREDIENTS

2 LARGE PAPAYAS
2 LIMES
115 G/4 OZ CASTER SUGAR
150 ML/5 FL OZ COLD WATER
1 TBSP WHITE RUM (OPTIONAL)

METHOD

● Peel the papayas and scoop out the seeds. Chop the fruit into chunks 2 cm/¾ in square. ● Put the sugar and water in a saucepan, place over a low heat and stir until the sugar has dissolved. ● Bring the syrup to the boil and boil without stirring for 5 minutes, then leave until cool. ● Weigh out 450 g/1 lb of the papaya and place it in a blender. (Keep any leftover fruit, chop into smaller dice, chill and serve with the sorbet). ● Add the syrup to the fruit in the blender and process until a smooth pulp forms. ● Squeeze the limes and add the juice and rum, if using, to the pulp. Mix well and transfer to a plastic freezerproof container. ● Freeze for 2 hours or until semi-frozen. Remove from the freezer, empty into a bowl and whisk with an electric whisk. ● Return the mixture to the container and freeze for another 2 hours. ● Repeat the beating process, then freeze for another 2 hours or until you are ready to serve.

PREPARATION TIME: 45 MINUTES
FREEZING TIME: 6 HOURS

TIP

If you add the rum, the sorbet will set less hard and should be served as soon as it is taken out of the freezer.

ORANGE BOATS

Once a cliché of the 1970s dinner table, there's something rather charming and nostalgic about these orange sorbets served in the hollowed-out shells of oranges, complete with their lids. The egg white adds a little texture and lightness to the sorbet.

INGREDIENTS

4 LARGE ORANGES
1 CARTON OF FRESHLY SQUEEZED ORANGE JUICE
450 ML/16 FL OZ COLD WATER, PLUS 3 TBSP
225 G/8 OZ GRANULATED SUGAR
3 TSP POWDERED GELATINE
2 LARGE EGG WHITES

METHOD

● Cut the tops off the oranges and work around the inside of the skin to cut out the flesh. Set the skins aside. ● Squeeze the orange pieces into a jug to extract the juice. You will need 450 ml/16 fl oz; if you don't have enough, make up with juice from the carton. ● Put the sugar and water into a pan, place over a low heat and stir until the sugar has dissolved. Bring to the boil and boil for 10 minutes, without stirring, then cool. ● Put the remaining water into a heatproof bowl and sprinkle over the gelatine. Set over a pan of simmering water and leave for 5 minutes. ● Beat the gelatine and juice into the syrup, then pour into a freezerproof container and freeze for 1 hour. ● Beat the egg whites until stiff. ● Remove from the freezer and whisk in the egg whites. Freeze for 1 hour. ● Whisk the sorbet, then spoon into the skins; replace the lids. Freeze for 3 hours until solid.

PREPARATION TIME: 1 HOUR
FREEZING TIME: 5 HOURS

APPLE SNAP

The apple schnapps stops this sorbet from freezing too hard. It also offers the classic blackberry/apple combination that makes such a successful ice cream on pages 54–5. If you like, make both recipes and serve a scoop of each alongside a tuile (see pages 108–9).

INGREDIENTS

700 G/1 LB 9 OZ RIPE BLACKBERRIES
450 G/1 LB CASTER SUGAR
1 LEMON
3 TBSP APPLE SCHNAPPS

METHOD

● Preheat the oven to 180°C/350°F/Gas Mark 4 ● Put the blackberries and sugar into an ovenproof casserole dish. ● Squeeze the lemon and add 2 tablespoons of the juice to the blackberries. Stir well, cover and bake for 30 minutes until stewed. ● Remove from the oven and let them cool slightly. ● Transfer the fruit to a blender and blitz for 10 seconds until a purée forms. ● Rub the purée through a sieve into a large bowl, pushing through as much of the mixture as you can with a wooden spoon. Discard the pips left in the sieve. ● Stir in the schnapps, mixing thoroughly, then pour the sorbet into a plastic freezerproof container and freeze for 1 hour. ● Remove from the freezer and whisk well, then return to the freezer for another hour before repeating the process. ● After the mixture has been whisked twice, return to the freezer for at least 3 hours before serving. ● Remove the sorbet from the freezer just before you want to serve it.

PREPARATION TIME: 1 HOUR
FREEZING TIME: 5–6 HOURS

CHOC SORBET

Chocolate sorbet is one of those ideas that you'll either love or loath. Even if you suspect you might not like it, don't make up your mind until you've tried this recipe. It delivers a true, deep chocolate flavour and is amazingly rich for a water-based ice.

INGREDIENTS

115 G/4 OZ BITTER CHOCOLATE (AT LEAST 70% COCOA SOLIDS)
115 G/4 OZ CASTER SUGAR
55 G/2 OZ COCOA POWDER
600 ML/1 PINT COLD WATER

METHOD

● Chop the chocolate into small pieces with a sharp knife on a wooden chopping board. ● Put the sugar and cocoa powder into a saucepan and add the water. Place over a low heat and stir constantly until the sugar and cocoa have dissolved. ● Turn the heat down and simmer for 5 minutes. ● Remove from the heat, tip in the chopped chocolate pieces and stir thoroughly until the chocolate has melted. ● Leave the mixture to cool for 30 minutes. ● Pour the cooled, thickened chocolate syrup into a plastic freezerproof container and freeze for 2 hours. ● Remove from the freezer, stir thoroughly, then return to the freezer for another 2 hours. ● Remove from the freezer again and whisk the mixture gently until any solid ice around the edges has been amalgamated into the freezing syrup. ● Return to the freezer and leave to freeze for another 2 hours or until solid. ● Remove the sorbet from the freezer just before serving.

PREPARATION TIME: 40 MINUTES
FREEZING TIME: 6 HOURS

ICED ALASKA

Baked Alaska is a retro treat that doesn't often appear on a menu today – serve this home-made iced version to friends, and you are guaranteed plenty of oohing and aahing as it's brought to the table.

INGREDIENTS

**1 QUANTITY LEMON CURD ICE CREAM
(SEE PAGES 60–1)
1 SUBSTANTIAL CAKE BASE
(SEE PAGES 120–21)**

**FOR THE MERINGUE:
3 LARGE EGG WHITES
115 G/4 OZ CASTER SUGAR**

METHOD

● Make the lemon curd ice cream according to the recipe on page 60. Freeze it in a lined, deep 20-cm/8-in diameter cake tin. ● Make the cake base, but halve the quantities. ● About 30 minutes before serving, preheat the oven to 230°C/450°F/Gas Mark 8, line a baking tray with baking parchment and place the cooked cake base on it. ● Beat the egg whites until stiff, then beat in the sugar, a spoonful at a time, until the mixture has formed a glossy meringue. ● Remove the ice cream from the freezer, take it out of the tin and peel off the baking parchment. Place the ice cream on top of the cake base. ● Working quickly, cover with the meringue. ● Bake for 5–7 minutes until browned, then serve.

PREPARATION TIME: WITH PRE-MADE ICE CREAM & CAKE 30 MINUTES

LIME & GINGER

This refresher is neither a drink nor a sorbet, but a mixture between the two. It's not hard frozen but rather soft and slushy, ready to be scooped into glasses and served with long spoons.

INGREDIENTS

85 G/3 OZ FRESH ROOT GINGER
175 G/6 OZ GRANULATED SUGAR
600 ML/1 PINT COLD WATER
8 LIMES
2 TRAYS OF ICE CUBES

METHOD

● Peel the ginger and chop finely. ● Put the ginger pieces, sugar and water into a large saucepan, place over a low heat and stir until the sugar has completely dissolved. ● Increase the heat slightly and cook, without stirring, for 10 minutes. Remove from the heat and leave to cool. ● When the ginger syrup is completely cool, strain it into a bowl and discard the ginger pieces. Leave to chill until cold. ● Squeeze the limes, add the juice to the cold syrup and stir. ● Pour the lime-and-ginger syrup into a blender and add the ice cubes (the blender should be filled two-thirds full – don't overfill it, or your refresher won't mix properly). ● Blitz in short bursts until the ice has been pulverized into a coarse ice 'snow', and the ginger and lime are thoroughly mixed. You may have to stir the mixture in the blender goblet halfway through

PREPARATION TIME: 1 HOUR
NO FREEZING TIME, BUT YOU NEED
READYMADE ICE

to make sure that everything is properly amalgamated. ● Pour the refresher into tall glasses or large tumblers and serve with long spoons, so that you can alternately sip and scoop the ginger and lime ice.

TIP

The ginger syrup that is used as its base can be kept in the fridge for up to a week. In hot weather, it's worth doubling the amount and saving half to use on another day.

APPLE HONEY

Made with a mixture of whole stewed apples and apple juice, this water ice has a wonderful flavour that is enhanced by a slight accent of honey. Choose a clear honey that doesn't have an overwhelming topnote, such as 'wildflower' honey.

INGREDIENTS

1 LITRE/1¾ PINTS ORGANIC APPLE JUICE
700 G/1 LB 9 OZ EATING APPLES
140 G/5 OZ GRANULATED SUGAR
2 TBSP CLEAR HONEY

METHOD

● Pour the apple juice into a heavy-based saucepan and bring to the boil over a medium heat. Turn the heat down and leave to simmer for 20 minutes or until the quantity has reduced by about half. ● While the apple juice is reducing, peel and core the apples and cut them into small chunks. ● Add the sugar and peeled apples to the reduced juice and cook over a low heat until the apple chunks are soft and beginning to break up. ● Stir the honey into the apple mixture and leave to cool. ● When the mixture is cold, pour it into a blender and blitz for a few 5-second bursts until a smooth purée forms. ● Pour the purée into a plastic freezerproof container and freeze for 1 hour. ● Remove from the freezer and whisk well to break up any ice crystals. ● Return to the freezer and freeze for another hour. Repeat the whisking process, before leaving to freeze for about 3 hours or until solid. ● Remove from the freezer and set aside for 5 minutes before serving.

PREPARATION TIME: 1 HOUR
FREEZING TIME: 5 HOURS

CHAMPAGNE

The perfect celebration drink-cum-dessert, this sorbet tastes uninhibitedly luxurious. There's no need to use vintage champagne, and there'll be some left over to enjoy while the sorbet freezes and you wait for your guests to arrive.

INGREDIENTS

225 G/8 OZ CASTER SUGAR
300 ML/10 FL OZ COLD WATER
2 ORANGES
300 ML/10 FL OZ CHAMPAGNE
FRESH RASPBERRIES, TO SERVE

METHOD

● Put the sugar and water into a saucepan, place over a low heat and stir until the sugar has dissolved. Remove from the heat and leave to cool. ● Squeeze the oranges into a small bowl. ● Pour the champagne and the orange juice into the cooled sugar syrup and stir to combine. ● Pour the mixture into a plastic freezerproof container and freeze for 2 hours. ● Remove the sorbet from the freezer, empty it into a blender and blend for 5 seconds. Return the sorbet to the container and freeze for another 2 hours. ● Repeat the process twice more. After the third re-mixing you can leave the sorbet to freeze undisturbed for 4 hours or overnight. Because of the alcohol content it will not freeze very hard. ● Remove the sorbet from the freezer just before serving. It looks pretty with a few fresh raspberries scattered over the top.

PREPARATION TIME: 20 MINUTES
FREEZING TIME: 8 HOURS

MELON SORBET

The refreshing sweetness and subtle flavour of cantaloupe melon, lifted with a hint of tart lime juice, work together to make an excellent sorbet. If what you want at the end of a meal is a palate-cleanser instead of a rich dessert, then this is the perfect solution.

INGREDIENTS

1 CANTALOUPE MELON, AS RIPE AS POSSIBLE
1 LIME
55 G/2 OZ ICING SUGAR
1 LARGE EGG WHITE

METHOD

● Cut the melon into thick wedges, deseed, then slice the fruit away from the skin and cut into chunks. ● Squeeze the lime, put the juice into a bowl and add the icing sugar. Stir to combine. ● Put the lime juice and the melon pieces into a blender and blitz in 5-second bursts until a smooth purée forms. ● Pour the melon mixture into a plastic freezerproof container and freeze for 1½ hours. ● Put the egg white in a bowl and beat until stiff. ● Remove the half-frozen melon mixture from the freezer and empty it into a bowl. Whisk briefly to break up any ice crystals, then whisk in the beaten egg white. ● Return the sorbet to the container and freeze until firm (this will take about 3 hours). ● Remove the sorbet from the freezer just before serving.

PREPARATION TIME: 10 MINUTES
FREEZING TIME: 4 HOURS 30 MINUTES

CHAPTER 4
ACCOMPANIMENTS

What you serve with ice cream can be almost as important as the ice cream itself. There are some perfect natural partnerships – few accompaniments go as well with stem-ginger ice cream as a crisp meringue, for instance, and lemon or strawberry ice cream tastes particularly good with a wedge of crunchy, citrus shortbread. Other accompaniments will complement almost anything – if you like chocolate sauce, you may well enjoy it as much with a semifreddo as with a vanilla ice, and most fruit ices will be enhanced by a drizzle of sticky melba sauce. But, whatever your taste, if you want to dress up a plainish ice cream as a formal dessert, the following recipes provide some mouthwatering choices.

BROWNIES

The ultimate complement to a scoop of vanilla ice cream, the best brownies are fudgy, rich, and intensely chocolatey. This recipe satisfies on all counts – although it is made with cocoa rather than pure chocolate, it delivers 12 brownies with a strong chocolate hit.

INGREDIENTS

115 G/4 OZ UNSALTED BUTTER
250 G/9 OZ CASTER SUGAR
2 LARGE EGGS
55 G/2 OZ COCOA POWDER
55 G/2 OZ PLAIN FLOUR

YOU WILL ALSO NEED A 30 X 10-CM/12 X 4-IN LONG TART TIN LINED WITH FOIL. YOU CAN USE ANY SIMILARLY SIZED TIN, SO LONG AS IT IS MORE THAN 2.5 CM/1 IN DEEP AND NOT TOO LARGE – THE MIXTURE SHOULD BE 2.5 CM/1 IN DEEP WHEN IT IS POURED INTO THE TIN.

METHOD

● Preheat the oven to 180°C/350°F/Gas Mark 4. ● Put the butter into a small saucepan and place over a low heat to melt. ● While the butter is melting, put the sugar in a large bowl, add the eggs and whisk together for 2–3 minutes until the mixture is thick, light and pale. ● When the butter has melted, remove from the heat and, using a wooden spoon, stir in the cocoa powder, mixing thoroughly. Pour into the sugar-and-egg mixture and whisk together to combine. ● Add the flour to the mixture and whisk again. When everything is well mixed, use a wooden spatula to help you pour the mixture into the prepared tin. ● Bake on the middle shelf of the oven for about 25 minutes or

PREPARATION TIME: ABOUT 10 MINUTES
COOKING TIME: ABOUT 25 MINUTES

until the top is solid and slightly cracked and the tip of a knife inserted into the mixture comes out sticky. ● Remove from the oven and leave to cool in the tin. ● When the brownies are cool, remove from the tin, peel off the foil and cut into 12 squares.

TIP

For the best taste, choose the highest-quality cocoa you can find. You can add chopped nuts or chocolate chips, according to taste, but try the recipe plain first – it's delicious.

NUT TOPPING

Praline is nothing more than nut toffee pulverized into a delicious crunchy rubble. It makes a great topping for almost any ice cream, or can be stirred through a plain vanilla ice to give it a little crunch.

INGREDIENTS

140 G/5 OZ CASTER SUGAR
90 ML/3 FL OZ COLD WATER
115 G/4 OZ FLAKED ALMONDS

YOU WILL ALSO NEED A GREASED BAKING TRAY

METHOD

● Put the sugar and water into a saucepan, place the pan over a low heat and stir occasionally until the sugar has dissolved. ● Increase the heat slightly and keep it over a steady heat, shaking the pan every few minutes, for 10–15 minutes until the colour gradually becomes darker. When it deepens to a mid-caramel, remove the saucepan from the heat and mix in the flaked almonds. ● Pour onto a greased baking tray and leave until completely cold. ● Break the praline into pieces (if you want a fine texture, crush it with a rolling pin between 2 sheets of greaseproof paper) and store in an airtight jar until you want to use it.

PREPARATION AND COOKING TIME:
ABOUT 20 MINUTES

SUNDAE SAUCE

A luxurious touch to turn plain ice cream into something more like a sundae, this butterscotch sauce may be a little too sugary for any non-sweet-toothed grown-ups, but it is usually a big hit with children.

INGREDIENTS

85 G/3 OZ UNSALTED BUTTER
115 G/4 OZ SOFT BROWN SUGAR
115 G/4 OZ MUSCOVADO SUGAR
150 ML/5 FL OZ DOUBLE CREAM
1 TBSP GOLDEN SYRUP

METHOD

● Melt the butter in a small saucepan over a low heat. ● Add both sugars, the cream and golden syrup and stir to mix. ● When the sugars have completely dissolved, increase the heat slightly and bring the sauce to the boil. ● Allow it to boil for 1 minute, then remove from the heat and leave to cool. ● The sauce can either be served warm or chilled (if allowed to go completely cold it will become much thicker).

PREPARATION AND COOKING TIME:
ABOUT 10 MINUTES

COOKIES

If you don't regard the brownie as the natural partner to a scoop of vanilla, chances are that the chocolate chip cookie occupies that particular place in your pantheon. This recipe should meet the need; it makes 20 small or 10 huge cookies.

INGREDIENTS

115 G/4 OZ PLAIN CHOCOLATE
115 G/4 OZ UNSALTED BUTTER, SOFTENED AND CUT INTO CUBES
115 G/4 OZ CASTER SUGAR
115 G/4 OZ SOFT BROWN SUGAR
1 LARGE EGG
115 G/4 OZ PLAIN FLOUR
½ TSP BAKING POWDER

**YOU WILL ALSO NEED 2 BAKING TRAYS,
GREASED OR LINED WITH BAKING PARCHMENT**

METHOD

● Preheat the oven to 180°C/350°F/Gas Mark 4. ● Put the butter into a large bowl. ● Chop the chocolate into small pieces, about the size of peas. ● Add both sugars to the butter and beat together until soft and fluffy, then beat in the egg and, finally, the flour and baking powder. Stir in the chocolate. ● Drop tablespoons (for the large size) or heaped teaspoons (for smaller cookies) onto the prepared baking trays, leaving enough room around each for the cookies to spread. ● Bake for 10 minutes until lightly browned at the edges but still soft. Leave to cool for 10 minutes before transferring to wire racks to crisp up.

PREPARATION TIME: 15 MINUTES
COOKING TIME: 10 MINUTES

CHOC SAUCE

This sauce is very rich, but utterly delicious – it tastes like the essence of chocolate. It goes with the most adult flavours: pistachio, chestnut, ginger and, of course, vanilla.

INGREDIENTS

200 G/7 OZ PLAIN CHOCOLATE
(AT LEAST 60% COCOA SOLIDS)
2 TBSP HOT WATER
85 G/3 OZ CASTER SUGAR
150 ML/5 FL OZ DOUBLE CREAM

METHOD

● Break the chocolate into pieces and put into a small, heavy-based saucepan. Add the hot water and place the saucepan over a very low heat. As it starts to melt, add the sugar and stir gently. ● When the chocolate has melted and combined with the sugar, gradually stir in the cream. Simmer the sauce gently for 5 minutes, but do not allow it to boil. ● The sauce is now ready to use but leave it to cool slightly before serving. It also works as a cold sauce but thickens considerably as it cools, giving a more fudgy result.

PREPARATION AND COOKING TIME:
15 MINUTES

106

TOFFEE SAUCE

Hardly a recipe, this sauce is invariably popular and very, very speedy. When you've mastered the Mars bar variety, you can experiment with other favourite chocolate bars: any toffee-and-chocolate mixture tends to be good, but Toblerone and Snickers have their devotees, too.

INGREDIENTS

2 REGULAR SIZE MARS BARS
3 TBSP FULL-CREAM MILK

METHOD

● Using a sharp knife and a chopping board, chop the Mars bars into slices 1 cm/½ in thick. ● Place the Mars bar pieces into a small, heavy-based saucepan and pour in the milk. ● Heat very gently, stirring to combine. After 2–3 minutes you will have a very thick and milky chocolate-and-toffee sauce.

PREPARATION AND COOKING TIME:
5 MINUTES

TUILES

These curvy little almond biscuits are a classic accompaniment to creamy desserts and pair particularly well with fruit-flavoured ices and sorbets. Despite their fragile look they're not hard to make, although creating the characteristic curl can take a little practice.

INGREDIENTS

55 G/2 OZ UNSALTED BUTTER, SOFTENED
115 G/4 OZ CASTER SUGAR
115 G/4 OZ FLAKED ALMONDS
25 G/1 OZ PLAIN FLOUR
½ TSP VANILLA EXTRACT

YOU WILL ALSO NEED 2 BAKING TRAYS, GREASED OR LINED WITH BAKING PARCHMENT, AND ONE OR MORE WOODEN SPOONS

METHOD

● Preheat the oven to 200°C/400°F/Gas Mark 6 ● Put the butter and sugar in a large bowl and beat together with a wooden spoon until fluffy. ● Beat in the almonds, then the flour and then the vanilla extract. ● Drop 10–12 small spoonfuls of the mixture onto the prepared baking tray, then use the edge of the wooden spoon to pull them out a little into thin circles. Leave room around each tuile for the mixture to spread out. ● Bake for about 10 minutes but check the tuiles after 5 minutes – as soon as the biscuits are golden brown they are ready. ● Remove from the oven and cool for a minute, but no longer. Then, working quickly and carefully, slide a palette knife under one biscuit and gently drape it over a rolling pin. As it cools, it will set in a curve.

PREPARATION TIME: 15 MINUTES
COOKING TIME: 10 MINUTES

Repeat for every biscuit, removing the set ones to a wire rack as you go. • Unless you are eating the tuiles straight away, transfer them to an airtight container when they are completely cool.

TIP

Real virtuosos can make tuile-biscuit cones and cups by dextrously hanging the warm biscuits over the bases of egg cups or slightly larger cups, but try the simple curled shape first.

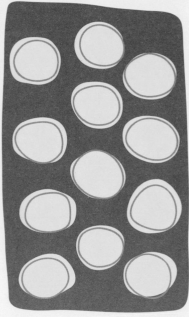

AFFOGATTO

This coffee-and-ice-cream combo is less of a recipe than what old-fashioned food packaging used to call 'a serving suggestion', although it's one that is a popular snack in Italy. You need an espresso machine to make it properly – no substitute will do for this recipe.

INGREDIENTS

1–2 SCOOPS OF HOME-MADE VANILLA ICE CREAM
A CUP OF FRESH, HOT ESPRESSO COFFEE

METHOD

● Put the ice cream in a bowl. ● Pour the espresso over it and eat with a small spoon. That's it, but the detail is important here. If you don't have an espresso machine, go to your best local Italian café and order the coffee and the ice cream separately, then combine them at table. Everyone should try this treat at least once.

PREPARATION TIME: 3 MINUTES

SHORTBREAD

The ground rice gives this lemon shortbread a good, crisp finish, and the subtle lemon flavour works well with most kinds of ice cream. It is baked in a traditional round, on a baking tray, so that the end result can simply be broken into triangular wedges.

INGREDIENTS

115 G/4 OZ UNSALTED BUTTER, SOFTENED
3 LEMONS
55 G/2 OZ CASTER SUGAR
115 G/4 OZ PLAIN FLOUR
55 G/2 OZ GROUND RICE

YOU WILL ALSO NEED A LIGHTLY GREASED BAKING TRAY

METHOD

● Preheat the oven to 180°C/350°F/Gas Mark 4. ● Put the butter in a bowl and beat with a wooden spoon until soft and light. ● Zest the lemons, using either a purpose-made lemon zester or the fine side of an ordinary grater, and add the zest and sugar to the butter. Beat together until fluffy. ● Sift the flour and ground rice together in a separate bowl, then mix into the butter and sugar mixture until a soft dough forms. ● Flour your hands and form the dough into a ball, then place it on a wooden board and use a rolling pin to make it into a neat 16-cm/7-in round. ● Put the shortbread on the prepared baking tray and pinch around the edge of the round with your thumbs to give it the traditional-looking crimped edge. Prick at regular intervals with a fork and mark with a knife into 8 wedges. ● Bake on the middle

PREPARATION TIME: 10 MINUTES
COOKING TIME: 30 MINUTES

shelf of the oven for 30 minutes until the shortbread has turned a pale biscuit colour. ● Remove from the oven, ease onto a wire rack with a palette knife and leave to cool before breaking into triangles.

TIP

For an unorthodox but delicious summer birthday treat, you could also leave this shortbread in a round and pile it high with strawberry ice cream and fresh strawberries.

BRANDY SNAPS

The origins of these classic cylinders of lacy, ginger-scented biscuit have been much debated – chefs from Australia to Africa have claimed them for their own. What is unquestionable is that they make great partners for ice cream. There's no need to fill them with cream, either.

INGREDIENTS

40 G/1½ OZ UNSALTED BUTTER
40 G/1½ OZ CASTER SUGAR
2 TBSP GOLDEN SYRUP
½ TSP GROUND GINGER
40 G/1½ OZ PLAIN FLOUR
1 TSP BRANDY

YOU WILL ALSO NEED 2 BAKING TRAYS, GREASED OR LINED WITH BAKING PARCHMENT

METHOD

● Preheat the oven to 180°C/350°F/Gas Mark 4. ● Put the butter and sugar into a small saucepan and add the golden syrup. Melt together gently, then stir until the mixture is combined. Remove from the heat. ● Sift the ground ginger and flour into the melted butter mixture, then pour in the brandy. Stir briefly but thoroughly, then drop 8–10 small spoonfuls of the mixture onto the prepared baking trays, leaving enough room for the snaps to spread during cooking. ● Bake in the middle of the oven for 5 minutes or until they turn a deeper brown. ● Take one tray out of the oven and, working quickly, lift a snap with a palette knife and neatly curl it around the handle of a wooden spoon. As soon as the biscuits start to set, they can be removed from the

PREPARATION AND COOKING TIME:
ABOUT 15 MINUTES

114

wooden spoons and transferred to a wire rack to cool. Continue until you have rolled all the brandy snaps. These biscuits are most delicious eaten soon after making, but they can be kept in an airtight container for a day or two if necessary.

TIP

This recipe makes quite a small quantity – 8 to 10 snaps – because you have to work quickly while the biscuits are still warm to get the cylindrical shape. When you've had a little practice, you can increase the quantity.

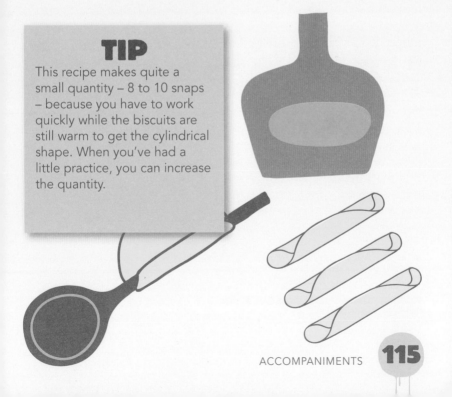

CINDER TOFFEE

Variously known as cinder, honeycomb or bonfire toffee, this traditional sweet marries well with any of the plainer creamy ices – either broken into small pieces and swirled through the mixture to supply delectable bits of crunchiness or crushed and scattered over the top.

INGREDIENTS

500 G/1 LB 2 OZ GRANULATED SUGAR
4 TBSP WHITE VINEGAR
300 ML/10 FL OZ COLD WATER
½ TSP BICARBONATE OF SODA

YOU WILL ALSO NEED A GREASED 30 X 10-CM/12 X 4-IN BAKING TIN

METHOD

● Put the sugar, vinegar and water into a large, heavy-based saucepan. Place the pan over a low heat and stir occasionally until all the sugar has dissolved and it is smooth. ● Increase the heat slightly and bring the syrup to the boil. Continue boiling, without stirring, over a medium heat until it reaches 149°C/300°F on a sugar thermometer. If you do not have a sugar thermometer, the toffee is ready when the colour has darkened slightly and when a small amount is dropped into a cup of cold water and forms a brittle little trail. ● When the mixture has reached this 'hard crack' stage, remove the pan from the heat and, covering your hand with a tea towel to prevent burning if the toffee spits, tip in the bicarbonate of soda. The mixture will foam up dramatically at this point (that's why you need a large pan for a comparatively small

PREPARATION AND COOKING TIME:
ABOUT 20 MINUTES

amount of toffee) and then subside slightly. Pour it immediately into the prepared tin and leave to set. ● After 5 minutes use a sharp knife to score the top into squares. This will make it easier to break into pieces when the toffee is set. ● When the toffee is completely cold, break it into pieces and store in an airtight container until ready to use.

TIP

When the toffee has cooled, put it into an airtight container immediately, otherwise it will quickly go soft and lose its alluring crunch. Once boxed, it will keep for a week or two.

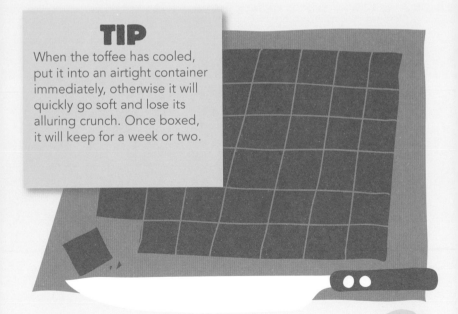

MACAROONS

Like meringues, macaroons are a great way to use up spare egg whites – but they also make a good accompaniment to ice cream in their own right. They're infinitely versatile – you can make tiny macaroons in pastel colours, or you can make the more traditional larger ones.

INGREDIENTS

140 G/5 OZ GROUND ALMONDS
200 G/7 OZ CASTER SUGAR
2 LARGE EGG WHITES
1 TBSP PLAIN FLOUR
1 TSP ALMOND EXTRACT
SHEETS OF RICE PAPER

YOU WILL ALSO NEED 2 BAKING TRAYS. IT'S TRADITIONAL BUT NOT ESSENTIAL TO LINE THEM WITH EDIBLE RICE PAPER, BUT IF YOU CAN'T FIND RICE PAPER, SIMPLY GREASE THE TRAYS

METHOD

● Preheat the oven to 160°C/325°F/Gas Mark 3. ● Put the ground almonds and sugar in a large bowl and stir, mixing together thoroughly. ● Add the egg whites, then stir again (the mixture will look like a thick, grainy batter). ● Sprinkle in the flour and the almond extract and stir again. ● Transfer the mixture to a piping bag and pipe rounds onto the prepared baking trays. Macaroons spread a little, although not as dramatically as tuiles. You will get 10–12 macaroons from this quantity of mixture. ● Bake for 20 minutes. The macaroons will expand slightly and cracks will begin to appear on the tops. Don't leave them in the oven too long – a good home-made macaroon should still be slightly

PREPARATION TIME: 10 MINUTES
COOKING TIME: 20 MINUTES

soft in the middle. ● Leave to cool on a wire rack. If you're not eating them straight away, transfer to an airtight container when they are completely cooled.

Variations
- Pipe miniature macaroons and use a drop of food colouring to turn them pink or green.
- Add a few drops of espresso to the mixture for coffee macaroons and a drop or two of vanilla extract for vanilla ones.
- Try ½ teaspoon of cocoa powder to add a chocolate flavour.

LAYER CAKE

The ice cream for this sponge cake should be made in advance, but instead of freezing in a container, pour it into two 20-cm-/8-in-diameter sandwich tins lined with clingfilm. When the disks have frozen, remove from the tins, wrap in clingfilm and freeze until assembling the cake.

INGREDIENTS

175 G/6 OZ UNSALTED BUTTER, SOFTENED AND CUT INTO CUBES
175 G/6 OZ CASTER SUGAR
3 LARGE EGGS
175 G/6 OZ SELF-RAISING FLOUR
1 TSP BAKING POWDER
1 TSP VANILLA EXTRACT
CREAM, MAPLE SYRUP OR FRUIT COULIS, TO SERVE

YOU WILL ALSO NEED 3 GREASED AND FLOURED 20-CM/8-IN DIAMETER SANDWICH CAKE TINS

METHOD

● Preheat the oven to 180°C/350°F/Gas Mark 4. ● Put the butter and sugar into a bowl and beat with an electric mixer until combined. Add the eggs, flour, baking powder and vanilla extract and beat together for 2 minutes until pale and light. ● Divide the mixture among the prepared tins and bake for about 15 minutes or until lightly browned and beginning to draw away from the sides of the tin. ● Turn the cake onto wire racks and leave to cool. ● To assemble, put one cake layer on a plate, unwrap a layer of ice cream and lay it on top, then add another layer each of cake and ice cream, finishing with the final layer of cake. Serve with cream, maple syrup or fruit coulis.

PREPARATION AND COOKING TIME:
ABOUT 40 MINUTES

MERINGUES

Many of the ice-cream recipes in the earlier chapters leave you with surplus egg whites. Meringues are breathtakingly speedy to mix, and they make such good partners for ice cream – unrecognizable different from the brittle whorls of commercially produced products.

INGREDIENTS

(TO MAKE 10 MEDIUM-SIZED MERINGUES)
2 LARGE EGGS WHITES
140 G/5 OZ GOLDEN CASTER SUGAR (YOU CAN USE ORDINARY WHITE SUGAR, BUT THE GOLDEN VARIETY WILL GIVE THE MERINGUES AN APPETIZING LIGHT-BROWN SHEEN)

YOU WILL ALSO NEED 2 BAKING TRAYS, LINED WITH LIGHTLY GREASED BAKING PARCHMENT

METHOD

● Preheat the oven to 140°C/275°F/Gas Mark 1. ● Put the egg whites in a bowl and whisk until stiff. ● Gradually beat in the sugar, a tablespoonful at a time, until the mixture has formed into a glossy meringue. ● If you have a piping bag, fit it with a plain nozzle, fill it with meringue and pipe it onto the prepared baking trays in neat swirls. If you don't have a bag, drop heaped tablespoons of the mixture onto the trays. ● Bake in the oven for 1 hour and 20 minutes. To check if they are done, pick one up, tap the underside, and if it is firm then it is ready. Turn the oven off, leaving the meringues in it. When they are completely cool, remove from the oven and put them in an airtight container until ready to use.

PREPARATION TIME: 10 MINUTES
COOKING TIME: 1 HOUR 20 MINUTES

Variations

Try a meringue cake, using 3 egg whites and 185 g/7½ oz sugar. Pipe two circles of meringue with a 20-cm/8-in diameter onto baking parchment and cook as above, then sandwich with a disk of ice cream of your favourite flavour of ice cream (see pages 120–21) in each.

TIP

You can make meringues with soft brown sugar for a caramel taste. It also means they will stay softer inside.

MELBA SAUCE

This raspberry sauce was originally created by the French chef Escoffier for the Australian opera singer Dame Nellie Melba. Provided that it's made with fresh raspberries it has an unbeatably vibrant taste, and it pairs well with a wide range of ice cream.

INGREDIENTS

450 G/1 LB FRESH RASPBERRIES
115 G/4 OZ CASTER SUGAR
2 TSP CORNFLOUR
125 ML/4 FL OZ REDCURRANT JELLY
2 TSP LEMON JUICE
1 TSP BRANDY OR COINTREAU (OPTIONAL)

METHOD

● Put the raspberries in a blender and briefly blitz until a purée forms. Rub the purée through a sieve into a bowl with a wooden spoon. Discard the pips left in the sieve. ● Put the sugar and cornflour into a separate heatproof bowl and mix together well, then stir into the raspberry purée. ● Add the redcurrant jelly, lemon juice and the liqueur, if using, and stir well. ● Set the bowl over a saucepan of simmering water and cook, stirring constantly, for 10 minutes. The sauce will thicken slightly. ● Leave to cool, then serve either warm or cold. It can be kept in the refrigerator for a week.

PREPARATION AND COOKING TIME:
ABOUT 20 MINUTES

ICE BOWL

Not strictly a recipe, perhaps, but an excellent finishing touch if you're serving home-made ice cream as part of a celebratory meal. You can make an ice bowl well in advance of the party and store it in the freezer, ready to fetch out when you're ready to serve your ice cream.

INGREDIENTS

2 PLASTIC OR STAINLESS-STEEL BOWLS, ONE SMALL ENOUGH TO FIT INSIDE THE OTHER LEAVING A GAP BROAD ENOUGH TO MAKE A SUBSTANTIAL 'WALL' OF ICE. (BOWLS OF 1 LITRE/1¾ PINTS AND 5-LITRE/10-PINT CAPACITIES ARE IDEAL, ALTHOUGH A 2-LITRE/3½-PINT BOWL WILL ALSO WORK FOR THE SMALLER SIZE – YOUR ICE BOWL WILL SIMPLY HAVE SLIGHTLY NARROWER WALLS.

A ROLL OF PARCEL TAPE, SOME SMALL FLOWERS, GRAPES OR LEMON, LIME OR ORANGE SLICES, TO DECORATE

METHOD

● Suspend the smaller bowl inside the larger one by holding the rims level with one another and stretching lengths of parcel tape between the 2 bowls, from the inside of the smaller bowl to the outer edge of the large one. Use 4 lengths of tape to hold the smaller bowl steady, leaving an even gap between the bowls all the way round. ● If you want to use decorations in the ice, it must be frozen in 2 stages. Pour enough cold water into the gap to come halfway up the sides of the smaller bowl. ● Drop small flowers or any other decoration you want in on top of the water and stand the bowl on a level surface in the freezer. Freeze overnight. ● The next day, take the bowl out of the freezer and

**PREPARATION AND COOKING TIME:
ABOUT 10 MINUTES**

126   ACCOMPANIMENTS

fill the gap between the bowls to the top. You can add a second layer of decorations – this will mean that the finished bowl has 2 rows of fruit or flowers, one halfway up and one around its rim. Place back in the freezer and leave to freeze overnight. ● Remove the bowls from the freezer, fill the sink with hot water, and dip the outer bowl in it briefly. Remove from the sink and pull gently, and the outer mould will come away To remove the inner mould, fill with hot water and quickly tip it out again, then pull the smaller bowl away from the ice bowl. ● Wrap the finished ice bowl in clingfilm and keep it in the freezer until you are ready to use it.

INDEX